MW00885574

Gratitude Journal

I Am Grateful

Date:

My day today was:

People I am grateful for:

The best part of the day was

I am grateful for my friend_____

I am grateful that _____ made me smile today because they_____

_____

I am grateful that _____ made me laugh today because they_____

_____

I am grateful that I accomplished_____

I am grateful that I had time to_____

I am grateful for overcoming_____

I am grateful that I am_____

I am greatful for the beautiful things I have seen today_____

_____

Lessons I learnt today:

How I shared my gratitude with others today:

Tomorrow I am looking forward to:

I Am Grateful

Date:

My day today was:

People I am grateful for:

The best part of the day was

I am grateful for my friend_____

I am grateful that _____ made me smile today because they_____

_____

I am grateful that _____ made me laugh today because they_____

_____

I am grateful that I accomplished_____

I am grateful that I had time to_____

I am grateful for overcoming_____

I am grateful that I am_____

I am greatful for the beautiful things I have seen today_____

_____

Lessons I learnt today:

How I shared my gratitude with others today:

Tomorrow I am looking forward to:

I Am Grateful

Date:

My day today was:

People I am grateful for:

The best part of the day was

I am grateful for my friend_____

I am grateful that _____ made me smile today because they_____

_____

I am grateful that _____ made me laugh today because they_____

_____

I am grateful that I accomplished_____

I am grateful that I had time to_____

I am grateful for overcoming_____

I am grateful that I am_____

I am greatful for the beautiful things I have seen today_____

_____

Lessons I learnt today:

How I shared my gratitude with others today:

Tomorrow I am looking forward to:

I Am Grateful

Date: _____

My day today was:

People I am grateful for:

The best part of the day was

I am grateful for my friend_____

I am grateful that _____ made me smile today because they_____

_____

I am grateful that _____ made me laugh today because they_____

_____

I am grateful that I accomplished_____

I am grateful that I had time to_____

I am grateful for overcoming_____

I am grateful that I am_____

I am greatful for the beautiful things I have seen today_____

_____

Lessons I learnt today:

How I shared my gratitude with others today:

Tomorrow I am looking forward to:

I Am Grateful

Date:

My day today was:

People I am grateful for:

The best part of the day was

I am grateful for my friend_____

I am grateful that _____ made me smile today because they_____
_____

I am grateful that _____ made me laugh today because they_____
_____

I am grateful that I accomplished_____

I am grateful that I had time to_____

I am grateful for overcoming_____

I am grateful that I am_____

I am greatful for the beautiful things I have seen today_____
_____

Lessons I learnt today:

How I shared my gratitude with others today:

Tomorrow I am looking forward to:

I Am Grateful

Date:

My day today was:

People I am grateful for:

The best part of the day was

I am grateful for my friend_____

I am grateful that _____ made me smile today because they_____

_____

I am grateful that _____ made me laugh today because they_____

_____

I am grateful that I accomplished_____

I am grateful that I had time to_____

I am grateful for overcoming_____

I am grateful that I am_____

I am greatful for the beautiful things I have seen today_____

_____

Lessons I learnt today:

How I shared my gratitude with others today:

Tomorrow I am looking forward to:

I Am Grateful

Date:

My day today was:

People I am grateful for:

The best part of the day was

I am grateful for my friend_____
I am grateful that _____ made me smile today because they_____
_____
I am grateful that _____ made me laugh today because they_____
_____
I am grateful that I accomplished_____
I am grateful that I had time to_____
I am grateful for overcoming_____
I am grateful that I am_____
I am greatful for the beautiful things I have seen today_____
_____

Lessons I learnt today:

How I shared my gratitude with others today:

Tomorrow I am looking forward to:

I Am Grateful

Date:

My day today was:

People I am grateful for:

The best part of the day was

I am grateful for my friend_____
I am grateful that _____ made me smile today because they_____
_____
I am grateful that _____ made me laugh today because they_____
_____
I am grateful that I accomplished_____
I am grateful that I had time to_____
I am grateful for overcoming_____
I am grateful that I am_____
I am greatful for the beautiful things I have seen today_____
_____

Lessons I learnt today:

How I shared my gratitude with others today:

Tomorrow I am looking forward to:

I Am Grateful

Date:

People I am grateful for:

My day today was:

The best part of the day was

I am grateful for my friend_____
I am grateful that _____ made me smile today because they_____
_____
I am grateful that _____ made me laugh today because they_____
_____
I am grateful that I accomplished_____
I am grateful that I had time to_____
I am grateful for overcoming_____
I am grateful that I am_____
I am greatful for the beautiful things I have seen today_____
_____

Lessons I learnt today:

How I shared my gratitude with others today:

Tomorrow I am looking forward to:

I Am Grateful

Date:

My day today was:

People I am grateful for:

The best part of the day was

I am grateful for my friend_____

I am grateful that _____ made me smile today because they_____

_____

I am grateful that _____ made me laugh today because they_____

_____

I am grateful that I accomplished_____

I am grateful that I had time to_____

I am grateful for overcoming_____

I am grateful that I am_____

I am greatful for the beautiful things I have seen today_____

_____

Lessons I learnt today:

How I shared my gratitude with others today:

Tomorrow I am looking forward to:

I Am Grateful

Date:

My day today was:

People I am grateful for:

The best part of the day was

I am grateful for my friend_____

I am grateful that _____ made me smile today because they_____

_____

I am grateful that _____ made me laugh today because they_____

_____

I am grateful that I accomplished_____

I am grateful that I had time to_____

I am grateful for overcoming_____

I am grateful that I am_____

I am greatful for the beautiful things I have seen today_____

_____

Lessons I learnt today:

How I shared my gratitude with others today:

Tomorrow I am looking forward to:

I Am Grateful

Date:

My day today was:

People I am grateful for:

The best part of the day was

I am grateful for my friend_____

I am grateful that _____ made me smile today because they_____

_____

I am grateful that _____ made me laugh today because they_____

_____

I am grateful that I accomplished_____

I am grateful that I had time to_____

I am grateful for overcoming_____

I am grateful that I am_____

I am greatful for the beautiful things I have seen today_____

_____

Lessons I learnt today:

How I shared my gratitude with others today:

Tomorrow I am looking forward to:

I Am Grateful

Date:

My day today was:

People I am grateful for:

The best part of the day was

I am grateful for my friend_____

I am grateful that _____ made me smile today because they_____
_____

I am grateful that _____ made me laugh today because they_____
_____

I am grateful that I accomplished_____

I am grateful that I had time to_____

I am grateful for overcoming_____

I am grateful that I am_____

I am greatful for the beautiful things I have seen today_____
_____

Lessons I learnt today:

How I shared my gratitude with others today:

Tomorrow I am looking forward to:

I Am Grateful

Date:

My day today was:

People I am grateful for:

The best part of the day was

I am grateful for my friend_____

I am grateful that _____ made me smile today because they_____

_____

I am grateful that _____ made me laugh today because they_____

_____

I am grateful that I accomplished_____

I am grateful that I had time to_____

I am grateful for overcoming_____

I am grateful that I am_____

I am greatful for the beautiful things I have seen today_____

_____

Lessons I learnt today:

How I shared my gratitude with others today:

Tomorrow I am looking forward to:

I Am Grateful

Date:

My day today was:

People I am grateful for:

The best part of the day was

I am grateful for my friend_____
I am grateful that _____ made me smile today because they_____
_____
I am grateful that _____ made me laugh today because they_____
_____
I am grateful that I accomplished_____
I am grateful that I had time to_____
I am grateful for overcoming_____
I am grateful that I am_____
I am greatful for the beautiful things I have seen today_____
_____

Lessons I learnt today:

How I shared my gratitude with others today:

Tomorrow I am looking forward to:

I Am Grateful

Date:

My day today was:

People I am grateful for:

The best part of the day was

I am grateful for my friend_____
I am grateful that _____ made me smile today because they_____
_____
I am grateful that _____ made me laugh today because they_____
_____
I am grateful that I accomplished_____
I am grateful that I had time to_____
I am grateful for overcoming_____
I am grateful that I am_____
I am greatful for the beautiful things I have seen today_____
_____

Lessons I learnt today:

How I shared my gratitude with others today:

Tomorrow I am looking forward to:

I Am Grateful

Date:

My day today was:

People I am grateful for:

The best part of the day was

I am grateful for my friend_____
I am grateful that _____ made me smile today because they_____
_____
I am grateful that _____ made me laugh today because they_____
_____
I am grateful that I accomplished_____
I am grateful that I had time to_____
I am grateful for overcoming_____
I am grateful that I am_____
I am greatful for the beautiful things I have seen today_____
_____

Lessons I learnt today:

How I shared my gratitude with others today:

Tomorrow I am looking forward to:

I Am Grateful

Date:

People I am grateful for:

My day today was:

The best part of the day was

I am grateful for my friend_____

I am grateful that _____ made me smile today because they_____

_____

I am grateful that _____ made me laugh today because they_____

_____

I am grateful that I accomplished_____

I am grateful that I had time to_____

I am grateful for overcoming_____

I am grateful that I am_____

I am greatful for the beautiful things I have seen today_____

_____

Lessons I learnt today:

How I shared my gratitude with others today:

Tomorrow I am looking forward to:

I Am Grateful

Date:

My day today was:

People I am grateful for:

The best part of the day was

I am grateful for my friend_____

I am grateful that _____ made me smile today because they_____

_____

I am grateful that _____ made me laugh today because they_____

_____

I am grateful that I accomplished_____

I am grateful that I had time to_____

I am grateful for overcoming_____

I am grateful that I am_____

I am greatful for the beautiful things I have seen today_____

_____

Lessons I learnt today:

How I shared my gratitude with others today:

Tomorrow I am looking forward to:

I Am Grateful

Date:

My day today was:

People I am grateful for:

The best part of the day was

I am grateful for my friend_____

I am grateful that _____ made me smile today because they_____

_____

I am grateful that _____ made me laugh today because they_____

_____

I am grateful that I accomplished_____

I am grateful that I had time to_____

I am grateful for overcoming_____

I am grateful that I am_____

I am greatful for the beautiful things I have seen today_____

_____

Lessons I learnt today:

How I shared my gratitude with others today:

Tomorrow I am looking forward to:

I Am Grateful

Date:

My day today was:

People I am grateful for:

The best part of the day was

I am grateful for my friend_____
I am grateful that _____ made me smile today because they_____
_____
I am grateful that _____ made me laugh today because they_____
_____
I am grateful that I accomplished_____
I am grateful that I had time to_____
I am grateful for overcoming_____
I am grateful that I am_____
I am greatful for the beautiful things I have seen today_____
_____

Lessons I learnt today:

How I shared my gratitude with others today:

Tomorrow I am looking forward to:

I Am Grateful

Date:

My day today was:

People I am grateful for:

The best part of the day was

I am grateful for my friend_____

I am grateful that _____ made me smile today because they_____

_____

I am grateful that _____ made me laugh today because they_____

_____

I am grateful that I accomplished_____

I am grateful that I had time to_____

I am grateful for overcoming_____

I am grateful that I am_____

I am greatful for the beautiful things I have seen today_____

_____

Lessons I learnt today:

How I shared my gratitude with others today:

Tomorrow I am looking forward to:

I Am Grateful

Date:

People I am grateful for:

My day today was:

The best part of the day was

I am grateful for my friend_____
I am grateful that _____ made me smile today because they_____
_____
I am grateful that _____ made me laugh today because they_____
_____
I am grateful that I accomplished_____
I am grateful that I had time to_____
I am grateful for overcoming_____
I am grateful that I am_____
I am greatful for the beautiful things I have seen today_____
_____

Lessons I learnt today:

How I shared my gratitude with others today:

Tomorrow I am looking forward to:

I Am Grateful

Date:

My day today was:

People I am grateful for:

The best part of the day was

I am grateful for my friend_____

I am grateful that _____ made me smile today because they_____

_____

I am grateful that _____ made me laugh today because they_____

I am grateful that I accomplished_____

I am grateful that I had time to_____

I am grateful for overcoming_____

I am grateful that I am_____

I am greatful for the beautiful things I have seen today_____

_____

Lessons I learnt today:

How I shared my gratitude with others today:

Tomorrow I am looking forward to:

I Am Grateful

Date:

People I am grateful for:

My day today was:

The best part of the day was

I am grateful for my friend_____
I am grateful that _____ made me smile today because they_____
_____
I am grateful that _____ made me laugh today because they_____
_____

I am grateful that I accomplished_____
I am grateful that I had time to_____
I am grateful for overcoming_____
I am grateful that I am_____
I am greatful for the beautiful things I have seen today_____
_____

Lessons I learnt today:

How I shared my gratitude with others today:

Tomorrow I am looking forward to:

I Am Grateful

Date:

My day today was:

People I am grateful for:

The best part of the day was

I am grateful for my friend_____
I am grateful that _____ made me smile today because they_____
_____
I am grateful that _____ made me laugh today because they_____
_____

I am grateful that I accomplished_____
I am grateful that I had time to_____
I am grateful for overcoming_____
I am grateful that I am_____
I am greatful for the beautiful things I have seen today_____
_____

Lessons I learnt today:

How I shared my gratitude with others today:

Tomorrow I am looking forward to:

I Am Grateful

Date:

My day today was:

People I am grateful for:

The best part of the day was

I am grateful for my friend_____

I am grateful that _____ made me smile today because they_____

_____

I am grateful that _____ made me laugh today because they_____

_____

I am grateful that I accomplished_____

I am grateful that I had time to_____

I am grateful for overcoming_____

I am grateful that I am_____

I am greatful for the beautiful things I have seen today_____

_____

Lessons I learnt today:

How I shared my gratitude with others today:

Tomorrow I am looking forward to:

I Am Grateful

Date:

My day today was:

People I am grateful for:

The best part of the day was

I am grateful for my friend_____

I am grateful that _____ made me smile today because they_____
_____

I am grateful that _____ made me laugh today because they_____
_____

I am grateful that I accomplished_____

I am grateful that I had time to_____

I am grateful for overcoming_____

I am grateful that I am_____

I am greatful for the beautiful things I have seen today_____
_____

Lessons I learnt today:

How I shared my gratitude with others today:

Tomorrow I am looking forward to:

I Am Grateful

Date:

My day today was:

People I am grateful for:

The best part of the day was

I am grateful for my friend_____

I am grateful that _____ made me smile today because they_____
_____

I am grateful that _____ made me laugh today because they_____
_____

I am grateful that I accomplished_____

I am grateful that I had time to_____

I am grateful for overcoming_____

I am grateful that I am_____

I am greatful for the beautiful things I have seen today_____
_____

Lessons I learnt today:

How I shared my gratitude with others today:

Tomorrow I am looking forward to:

I Am Grateful

Date:

My day today was:

People I am grateful for:

The best part of the day was

I am grateful for my friend_____
I am grateful that _____ made me smile today because they_____
_____
I am grateful that _____ made me laugh today because they_____
_____
I am grateful that I accomplished_____
I am grateful that I had time to_____
I am grateful for overcoming_____
I am grateful that I am_____
I am greatful for the beautiful things I have seen today_____
_____

Lessons I learnt today:

How I shared my gratitude with others today:

Tomorrow I am looking forward to:

I Am Grateful

Date:

My day today was:

People I am grateful for:

The best part of the day was

I am grateful for my friend_____
I am grateful that _____ made me smile today because they_____
_____
I am grateful that _____ made me laugh today because they_____

I am grateful that I accomplished_____
I am grateful that I had time to_____
I am grateful for overcoming_____
I am grateful that I am_____
I am greatful for the beautiful things I have seen today_____
_____

Lessons I learnt today:

How I shared my gratitude with others today:

Tomorrow I am looking forward to:

I Am Grateful

Date:

My day today was:

People I am grateful for:

The best part of the day was

I am grateful for my friend_____

I am grateful that _____ made me smile today because they_____

_____

I am grateful that _____ made me laugh today because they_____

_____

I am grateful that I accomplished_____

I am grateful that I had time to_____

I am grateful for overcoming_____

I am grateful that I am_____

I am greatful for the beautiful things I have seen today_____

_____

Lessons I learnt today:

How I shared my gratitude with others today:

Tomorrow I am looking forward to:

I Am Grateful

Date:

My day today was:

People I am grateful for:

The best part of the day was

I am grateful for my friend_____

I am grateful that _____ made me smile today because they_____

_____

I am grateful that _____ made me laugh today because they_____

_____

I am grateful that I accomplished_____

I am grateful that I had time to_____

I am grateful for overcoming_____

I am grateful that I am_____

I am greatful for the beautiful things I have seen today_____

_____

Lessons I learnt today:

How I shared my gratitude with others today:

Tomorrow I am looking forward to:

I Am Grateful

Date:

People I am grateful for:

My day today was:

The best part of the day was

I am grateful for my friend_____
I am grateful that _____ made me smile today because they_____
_____
I am grateful that _____ made me laugh today because they_____

_____
I am grateful that I accomplished_____
I am grateful that I had time to_____
I am grateful for overcoming_____
I am grateful that I am_____
I am greatful for the beautiful things I have seen today_____
_____

Lessons I learnt today:

How I shared my gratitude with others today:

Tomorrow I am looking forward to:

I Am Grateful

Date:

My day today was:

People I am grateful for:

The best part of the day was

I am grateful for my friend_____

I am grateful that _____ made me smile today because they_____

_____

I am grateful that _____ made me laugh today because they_____

_____

I am grateful that I accomplished_____

I am grateful that I had time to_____

I am grateful for overcoming_____

I am grateful that I am_____

I am greatful for the beautiful things I have seen today_____

_____

Lessons I learnt today:

How I shared my gratitude with others today:

Tomorrow I am looking forward to:

I Am Grateful

Date:

My day today was:

People I am grateful for:

The best part of the day was

I am grateful for my friend_____

I am grateful that _____ made me smile today because they_____
_____

I am grateful that _____ made me laugh today because they_____

_____

I am grateful that I accomplished_____
I am grateful that I had time to_____
I am grateful for overcoming_____
I am grateful that I am_____
I am greatful for the beautiful things I have seen today_____
_____

Lessons I learnt today:

How I shared my gratitude with others today:

Tomorrow I am looking forward to:

I Am Grateful

Date:

My day today was:

People I am grateful for:

The best part of the day was

I am grateful for my friend_____
I am grateful that _____ made me smile today because they_____
_____
I am grateful that _____ made me laugh today because they_____
_____
I am grateful that I accomplished_____
I am grateful that I had time to_____
I am grateful for overcoming_____
I am grateful that I am_____
I am greatful for the beautiful things I have seen today_____
_____

Lessons I learnt today:

How I shared my gratitude with others today:

Tomorrow I am looking forward to:

I Am Grateful

Date:

People I am grateful for:

My day today was:

The best part of the day was

I am grateful for my friend_____

I am grateful that _____ made me smile today because they_____

_____

I am grateful that _____ made me laugh today because they_____

_____

I am grateful that I accomplished_____

I am grateful that I had time to_____

I am grateful for overcoming_____

I am grateful that I am_____

I am greatful for the beautiful things I have seen today_____

_____

Lessons I learnt today:

How I shared my gratitude with others today:

Tomorrow I am looking forward to:

I Am Grateful

Date:

People I am grateful for:

My day today was:

The best part of the day was

I am grateful for my friend_____
I am grateful that _____ made me smile today because they_____
_____
I am grateful that _____ made me laugh today because they_____
_____
I am grateful that I accomplished_____
I am grateful that I had time to_____
I am grateful for overcoming_____
I am grateful that I am_____
I am greatful for the beautiful things I have seen today_____
_____

Lessons I learnt today:

How I shared my gratitude with others today:

Tomorrow I am looking forward to:

I Am Grateful

Date:

People I am grateful for:

My day today was:

The best part of the day was

I am grateful for my friend_____

I am grateful that _____ made me smile today because they_____

_____

I am grateful that _____ made me laugh today because they_____

_____

I am grateful that I accomplished_____

I am grateful that I had time to_____

I am grateful for overcoming_____

I am grateful that I am_____

I am greatful for the beautiful things I have seen today_____

_____

Lessons I learnt today:

How I shared my gratitude with others today:

Tomorrow I am looking forward to:

I Am Grateful

Date:

My day today was:

People I am grateful for:

The best part of the day was

I am grateful for my friend_____

I am grateful that _____ made me smile today because they_____
_____

I am grateful that _____ made me laugh today because they_____
_____

I am grateful that I accomplished_____

I am grateful that I had time to_____

I am grateful for overcoming_____

I am grateful that I am_____

I am greatful for the beautiful things I have seen today_____
_____

Lessons I learnt today:

How I shared my gratitude with others today:

Tomorrow I am looking forward to:

I Am Grateful

Date:

My day today was:

People I am grateful for:

The best part of the day was

I am grateful for my friend_____

I am grateful that _____ made me smile today because they_____

_____

I am grateful that _____ made me laugh today because they_____

_____

I am grateful that I accomplished_____

I am grateful that I had time to_____

I am grateful for overcoming_____

I am grateful that I am_____

I am greatful for the beautiful things I have seen today_____

_____

Lessons I learnt today:

How I shared my gratitude with others today:

Tomorrow I am looking forward to:

I Am Grateful

Date:

My day today was:

People I am grateful for:

The best part of the day was

I am grateful for my friend_____

I am grateful that _____ made me smile today because they_____

_____

I am grateful that _____ made me laugh today because they_____

_____

I am grateful that I accomplished_____

I am grateful that I had time to_____

I am grateful for overcoming_____

I am grateful that I am_____

I am greatful for the beautiful things I have seen today_____

_____

Lessons I learnt today:

How I shared my gratitude with others today:

Tomorrow I am looking forward to:

I Am Grateful

Date:

My day today was:

People I am grateful for:

The best part of the day was

I am grateful for my friend_____
I am grateful that _____ made me smile today because they_____
_____
I am grateful that _____ made me laugh today because they_____
_____
I am grateful that I accomplished_____
I am grateful that I had time to_____
I am grateful for overcoming_____
I am grateful that I am_____
I am greatful for the beautiful things I have seen today_____
_____

Lessons I learnt today:

How I shared my gratitude with others today:

Tomorrow I am looking forward to:

I Am Grateful

Date:

My day today was:

People I am grateful for:

The best part of the day was

I am grateful for my friend_____

I am grateful that _____ made me smile today because they_____
_____

I am grateful that _____ made me laugh today because they_____

_____

I am grateful that I accomplished_____

I am grateful that I had time to_____

I am grateful for overcoming_____

I am grateful that I am_____

I am greatful for the beautiful things I have seen today_____
_____

Lessons I learnt today:

How I shared my gratitude with others today:

Tomorrow I am looking forward to:

I Am Grateful

Date:

People I am grateful for:

My day today was:

The best part of the day was

I am grateful for my friend_____

I am grateful that _____ made me smile today because they_____

_____

I am grateful that _____ made me laugh today because they_____

_____

I am grateful that I accomplished_____

I am grateful that I had time to_____

I am grateful for overcoming_____

I am grateful that I am_____

I am greatful for the beautiful things I have seen today_____

_____

Lessons I learnt today:

How I shared my gratitude with others today:

Tomorrow I am looking forward to:

I Am Grateful

Date:

My day today was:

People I am grateful for:

The best part of the day was

I am grateful for my friend_____
I am grateful that _____ made me smile today because they_____
_____
I am grateful that _____ made me laugh today because they_____
_____

I am grateful that I accomplished_____
I am grateful that I had time to_____
I am grateful for overcoming_____
I am grateful that I am_____
I am greatful for the beautiful things I have seen today_____
_____

Lessons I learnt today:

How I shared my gratitude with others today:

Tomorrow I am looking forward to:

I Am Grateful

Date:

My day today was:

People I am grateful for:

The best part of the day was

I am grateful for my friend_____
I am grateful that _____ made me smile today because they_____
_____
I am grateful that _____ made me laugh today because they_____
_____

I am grateful that I accomplished_____
I am grateful that I had time to_____
I am grateful for overcoming_____
I am grateful that I am_____
I am greatful for the beautiful things I have seen today_____
_____

Lessons I learnt today:

How I shared my gratitude with others today:

Tomorrow I am looking forward to:

I Am Grateful

Date:

People I am grateful for:

My day today was:

The best part of the day was

I am grateful for my friend_____

I am grateful that _____ made me smile today because they_____

_____

I am grateful that _____ made me laugh today because they_____

_____

I am grateful that I accomplished_____

I am grateful that I had time to_____

I am grateful for overcoming_____

I am grateful that I am_____

I am greatful for the beautiful things I have seen today_____

_____

Lessons I learnt today:

How I shared my gratitude with others today:

Tomorrow I am looking forward to:

I Am Grateful

Date:

People I am grateful for:

My day today was:

The best part of the day was

I am grateful for my friend_____
I am grateful that _____ made me smile today because they_____
_____
I am grateful that _____ made me laugh today because they_____
_____

I am grateful that I accomplished_____
I am grateful that I had time to_____
I am grateful for overcoming_____
I am grateful that I am_____
I am greatful for the beautiful things I have seen today_____
_____

Lessons I learnt today:

How I shared my gratitude with others today:

Tomorrow I am looking forward to:

I Am Grateful

Date:

People I am grateful for:

My day today was:

The best part of the day was

I am grateful for my friend_____

I am grateful that _____ made me smile today because they_____
_____

I am grateful that _____ made me laugh today because they_____
_____

I am grateful that I accomplished_____

I am grateful that I had time to_____

I am grateful for overcoming_____

I am grateful that I am_____

I am greatful for the beautiful things I have seen today_____
_____

Lessons I learnt today:

How I shared my gratitude with others today:

Tomorrow I am looking forward to:

I Am Grateful

Date:

My day today was:

People I am grateful for:

The best part of the day was

I am grateful for my friend_____

I am grateful that _____ made me smile today because they_____

_____

I am grateful that _____ made me laugh today because they_____

_____

I am grateful that I accomplished_____

I am grateful that I had time to_____

I am grateful for overcoming_____

I am grateful that I am_____

I am greatful for the beautiful things I have seen today_____

_____

Lessons I learnt today:

How I shared my gratitude with others today:

Tomorrow I am looking forward to:

I Am Grateful

Date:

My day today was:

People I am grateful for:

The best part of the day was

I am grateful for my friend_____

I am grateful that _____ made me smile today because they_____

_____

I am grateful that _____ made me laugh today because they_____

_____

I am grateful that I accomplished_____

I am grateful that I had time to_____

I am grateful for overcoming_____

I am grateful that I am_____

I am greatful for the beautiful things I have seen today_____

_____

Lessons I learnt today:

How I shared my gratitude with others today:

Tomorrow I am looking forward to:

I Am Grateful

Date:

People I am grateful for:

My day today was:

The best part of the day was

I am grateful for my friend_____
I am grateful that _____ made me smile today because they_____
_____
I am grateful that _____ made me laugh today because they_____
_____
I am grateful that I accomplished_____
I am grateful that I had time to_____
I am grateful for overcoming_____
I am grateful that I am_____
I am greatful for the beautiful things I have seen today_____
_____

Lessons I learnt today:

How I shared my gratitude with others today:

Tomorrow I am looking forward to:

I Am Grateful

Date:

My day today was:

People I am grateful for:

The best part of the day was

I am grateful for my friend_____

I am grateful that _____ made me smile today because they_____

_____

I am grateful that _____ made me laugh today because they_____

_____

I am grateful that I accomplished_____

I am grateful that I had time to_____

I am grateful for overcoming_____

I am grateful that I am_____

I am greatful for the beautiful things I have seen today_____

_____

Lessons I learnt today:

How I shared my gratitude with others today:

Tomorrow I am looking forward to:

I Am Grateful

Date:

My day today was:

People I am grateful for:

The best part of the day was

I am grateful for my friend_____
I am grateful that _____ made me smile today because they_____
_____
I am grateful that _____ made me laugh today because they_____
_____
I am grateful that I accomplished_____
I am grateful that I had time to_____
I am grateful for overcoming_____
I am grateful that I am_____
I am greatful for the beautiful things I have seen today_____
_____

Lessons I learnt today:

How I shared my gratitude with others today:

Tomorrow I am looking forward to:

I Am Grateful

Date:

My day today was:

People I am grateful for:

The best part of the day was

I am grateful for my friend_____
I am grateful that _____ made me smile today because they_____
_____
I am grateful that _____ made me laugh today because they_____
_____
I am grateful that I accomplished_____
I am grateful that I had time to_____
I am grateful for overcoming_____
I am grateful that I am_____
I am greatful for the beautiful things I have seen today_____
_____

Lessons I learnt today:

How I shared my gratitude with others today:

Tomorrow I am looking forward to:

I Am Grateful

Date:

My day today was:

People I am grateful for:

The best part of the day was

I am grateful for my friend_____

I am grateful that _____ made me smile today because they_____

_____

I am grateful that _____ made me laugh today because they_____

_____

I am grateful that I accomplished_____

I am grateful that I had time to_____

I am grateful for overcoming_____

I am grateful that I am_____

I am greatful for the beautiful things I have seen today_____

_____

Lessons I learnt today:

How I shared my gratitude with others today:

Tomorrow I am looking forward to:

I Am Grateful

Date:

My day today was:

People I am grateful for:

The best part of the day was

I am grateful for my friend_____
I am grateful that _____ made me smile today because they_____
_____
I am grateful that _____ made me laugh today because they_____
_____
I am grateful that I accomplished_____
I am grateful that I had time to_____
I am grateful for overcoming_____
I am grateful that I am_____
I am greatful for the beautiful things I have seen today_____
_____

Lessons I learnt today:

How I shared my gratitude with others today:

Tomorrow I am looking forward to:

I Am Grateful

Date:

People I am grateful for:

My day today was:

The best part of the day was

I am grateful for my friend_____

I am grateful that _____ made me smile today because they_____

_____

I am grateful that _____ made me laugh today because they_____

_____

I am grateful that I accomplished_____

I am grateful that I had time to_____

I am grateful for overcoming_____

I am grateful that I am_____

I am greatful for the beautiful things I have seen today_____

_____

Lessons I learnt today:

How I shared my gratitude with others today:

Tomorrow I am looking forward to:

I Am Grateful

Date:

People I am grateful for:

My day today was:

The best part of the day was

I am grateful for my friend_____
I am grateful that _____ made me smile today because they_____
_____
I am grateful that _____ made me laugh today because they_____
_____
I am grateful that I accomplished_____
I am grateful that I had time to_____
I am grateful for overcoming_____
I am grateful that I am_____
I am greatful for the beautiful things I have seen today_____
_____

Lessons I learnt today:

How I shared my gratitude with others today:

Tomorrow I am looking forward to:

I Am Grateful

Date:

People I am grateful for:

My day today was:

The best part of the day was

I am grateful for my friend_____
I am grateful that _____ made me smile today because they_____
_____
I am grateful that _____ made me laugh today because they_____
_____
I am grateful that I accomplished_____
I am grateful that I had time to_____
I am grateful for overcoming_____
I am grateful that I am_____
I am greatful for the beautiful things I have seen today_____
_____

Lessons I learnt today:

How I shared my gratitude with others today:

Tomorrow I am looking forward to:

I Am Grateful

Date:

My day today was:

People I am grateful for:

The best part of the day was

I am grateful for my friend_____
I am grateful that _____ made me smile today because they_____
_____
I am grateful that _____ made me laugh today because they_____
_____
I am grateful that I accomplished_____
I am grateful that I had time to_____
I am grateful for overcoming_____
I am grateful that I am_____
I am greatful for the beautiful things I have seen today_____
_____

Lessons I learnt today:

How I shared my gratitude with others today:

Tomorrow I am looking forward to:

I Am Grateful

Date:

My day today was:

People I am grateful for:

The best part of the day was

I am grateful for my friend_____
I am grateful that _____ made me smile today because they_____
_____
I am grateful that _____ made me laugh today because they_____
_____
I am grateful that I accomplished_____
I am grateful that I had time to_____
I am grateful for overcoming_____
I am grateful that I am_____
I am greatful for the beautiful things I have seen today_____
_____

Lessons I learnt today:

How I shared my gratitude with others today:

Tomorrow I am looking forward to:

I Am Grateful

Date:

People I am grateful for:

My day today was:

The best part of the day was

I am grateful for my friend_____

I am grateful that _____ made me smile today because they_____

_____

I am grateful that _____ made me laugh today because they_____

_____

I am grateful that I accomplished_____

I am grateful that I had time to_____

I am grateful for overcoming_____

I am grateful that I am_____

I am greatful for the beautiful things I have seen today_____

_____

Lessons I learnt today:

How I shared my gratitude with others today:

Tomorrow I am looking forward to:

I Am Grateful

Date:

People I am grateful for:

My day today was:

The best part of the day was

I am grateful for my friend_____

I am grateful that _____ made me smile today because they_____

_____

I am grateful that _____ made me laugh today because they_____

_____

I am grateful that I accomplished_____

I am grateful that I had time to_____

I am grateful for overcoming_____

I am grateful that I am_____

I am greatful for the beautiful things I have seen today_____

_____

Lessons I learnt today:

How I shared my gratitude with others today:

Tomorrow I am looking forward to:

I Am Grateful

Date:

People I am grateful for:

My day today was:

The best part of the day was

I am grateful for my friend_____

I am grateful that _____ made me smile today because they_____

_____

I am grateful that _____ made me laugh today because they_____

_____

I am grateful that I accomplished_____

I am grateful that I had time to_____

I am grateful for overcoming_____

I am grateful that I am_____

I am greatful for the beautiful things I have seen today_____

_____

Lessons I learnt today:

How I shared my gratitude with others today:

Tomorrow I am looking forward to:

I Am Grateful

Date:

My day today was:

People I am grateful for:

The best part of the day was

I am grateful for my friend_____

I am grateful that _____ made me smile today because they_____

_____

I am grateful that _____ made me laugh today because they_____

_____

I am grateful that I accomplished_____

I am grateful that I had time to_____

I am grateful for overcoming_____

I am grateful that I am_____

I am greatful for the beautiful things I have seen today_____

_____

Lessons I learnt today:

How I shared my gratitude with others today:

Tomorrow I am looking forward to:

I Am Grateful

Date:

My day today was:

People I am grateful for:

The best part of the day was

I am grateful for my friend_____
I am grateful that _____ made me smile today because they_____
_____
I am grateful that _____ made me laugh today because they_____
_____
I am grateful that I accomplished_____
I am grateful that I had time to_____
I am grateful for overcoming_____
I am grateful that I am_____
I am greatful for the beautiful things I have seen today_____
_____

Lessons I learnt today:

How I shared my gratitude with others today:

Tomorrow I am looking forward to:

I Am Grateful

Date:

My day today was:

People I am grateful for:

The best part of the day was

I am grateful for my friend_____
I am grateful that _____ made me smile today because they_____
_____
I am grateful that _____ made me laugh today because they_____
_____
I am grateful that I accomplished_____
I am grateful that I had time to_____
I am grateful for overcoming_____
I am grateful that I am_____
I am greatful for the beautiful things I have seen today_____
_____

Lessons I learnt today:

How I shared my gratitude with others today:

Tomorrow I am looking forward to:

I Am Grateful

Date:

My day today was:

People I am grateful for:

The best part of the day was

I am grateful for my friend_____
I am grateful that _____ made me smile today because they_____
_____
I am grateful that _____ made me laugh today because they_____
_____
I am grateful that I accomplished_____
I am grateful that I had time to_____
I am grateful for overcoming_____
I am grateful that I am_____
I am greatful for the beautiful things I have seen today_____
_____

Lessons I learnt today:

How I shared my gratitude with others today:

Tomorrow I am looking forward to:

I Am Grateful

Date:

People I am grateful for:

My day today was:

The best part of the day was

I am grateful for my friend_____

I am grateful that _____ made me smile today because they_____

_____

I am grateful that _____ made me laugh today because they_____

_____

I am grateful that I accomplished_____

I am grateful that I had time to_____

I am grateful for overcoming_____

I am grateful that I am_____

I am greatful for the beautiful things I have seen today_____

_____

Lessons I learnt today:

How I shared my gratitude with others today:

Tomorrow I am looking forward to:

I Am Grateful

Date:

My day today was:

People I am grateful for:

The best part of the day was

I am grateful for my friend_____
I am grateful that _____ made me smile today because they_____
_____
I am grateful that _____ made me laugh today because they_____
_____
I am grateful that I accomplished_____
I am grateful that I had time to_____
I am grateful for overcoming_____
I am grateful that I am_____
I am greatful for the beautiful things I have seen today_____
_____

Lessons I learnt today:

How I shared my gratitude with others today:

Tomorrow I am looking forward to:

I Am Grateful

Date:

My day today was:

People I am grateful for:

The best part of the day was

I am grateful for my friend_____
I am grateful that _____ made me smile today because they_____
_____
I am grateful that _____ made me laugh today because they_____
_____
I am grateful that I accomplished_____
I am grateful that I had time to_____
I am grateful for overcoming_____
I am grateful that I am_____
I am greatful for the beautiful things I have seen today_____
_____

Lessons I learnt today:

How I shared my gratitude with others today:

Tomorrow I am looking forward to:

I Am Grateful

Date:

My day today was:

People I am grateful for:

The best part of the day was

I am grateful for my friend_____

I am grateful that _____ made me smile today because they_____

_____

I am grateful that _____ made me laugh today because they_____

_____

I am grateful that I accomplished_____

I am grateful that I had time to_____

I am grateful for overcoming_____

I am grateful that I am_____

I am greatful for the beautiful things I have seen today_____

_____

Lessons I learnt today:

How I shared my gratitude with others today:

Tomorrow I am looking forward to:

I Am Grateful

Date:

My day today was:

People I am grateful for:

The best part of the day was

I am grateful for my friend_____

I am grateful that _____ made me smile today because they_____

_____

I am grateful that _____ made me laugh today because they_____

_____

I am grateful that I accomplished_____

I am grateful that I had time to_____

I am grateful for overcoming_____

I am grateful that I am_____

I am greatful for the beautiful things I have seen today_____

_____

Lessons I learnt today:

How I shared my gratitude with others today:

Tomorrow I am looking forward to:

I Am Grateful

Date:

My day today was:

People I am grateful for:

The best part of the day was

I am grateful for my friend_____
I am grateful that _____ made me smile today because they_____
_____
I am grateful that _____ made me laugh today because they_____
_____
I am grateful that I accomplished_____
I am grateful that I had time to_____
I am grateful for overcoming_____
I am grateful that I am_____
I am greatful for the beautiful things I have seen today_____
_____

Lessons I learnt today:

How I shared my gratitude with others today:

Tomorrow I am looking forward to:

I Am Grateful

Date:

My day today was:

People I am grateful for:

The best part of the day was

I am grateful for my friend_____
I am grateful that _____ made me smile today because they_____
_____
I am grateful that _____ made me laugh today because they_____
_____
I am grateful that I accomplished_____
I am grateful that I had time to_____
I am grateful for overcoming_____
I am grateful that I am_____
I am greatful for the beautiful things I have seen today_____
_____

Lessons I learnt today:

How I shared my gratitude with others today:

Tomorrow I am looking forward to:

I Am Grateful

Date:

My day today was:

People I am grateful for:

The best part of the day was

I am grateful for my friend_____

I am grateful that _____ made me smile today because they_____
_____

I am grateful that _____ made me laugh today because they_____
_____

I am grateful that I accomplished_____

I am grateful that I had time to_____

I am grateful for overcoming_____

I am grateful that I am_____

I am greatful for the beautiful things I have seen today_____
_____

Lessons I learnt today:

How I shared my gratitude with others today:

Tomorrow I am looking forward to:

I Am Grateful

Date:

People I am grateful for:

My day today was:

The best part of the day was

I am grateful for my friend_____

I am grateful that _____ made me smile today because they_____

_____

I am grateful that _____ made me laugh today because they_____

_____

I am grateful that I accomplished_____

I am grateful that I had time to_____

I am grateful for overcoming_____

I am grateful that I am_____

I am greatful for the beautiful things I have seen today_____

_____

Lessons I learnt today:

How I shared my gratitude with others today:

Tomorrow I am looking forward to:

I Am Grateful

Date:

My day today was:

People I am grateful for:

The best part of the day was

I am grateful for my friend_____

I am grateful that _____ made me smile today because they_____

_____

I am grateful that _____ made me laugh today because they_____

_____

I am grateful that I accomplished_____

I am grateful that I had time to_____

I am grateful for overcoming_____

I am grateful that I am_____

I am greatful for the beautiful things I have seen today_____

_____

Lessons I learnt today:

How I shared my gratitude with others today:

Tomorrow I am looking forward to:

I Am Grateful

Date:

People I am grateful for:

My day today was:

The best part of the day was

I am grateful for my friend_____
I am grateful that _____ made me smile today because they_____
_____
I am grateful that _____ made me laugh today because they_____
_____
I am grateful that I accomplished_____
I am grateful that I had time to_____
I am grateful for overcoming_____
I am grateful that I am_____
I am greatful for the beautiful things I have seen today_____
_____

Lessons I learnt today:

How I shared my gratitude with others today:

Tomorrow I am looking forward to:

I Am Grateful

Date:

My day today was:

People I am grateful for:

The best part of the day was

I am grateful for my friend_____
I am grateful that _____ made me smile today because they_____
_____
I am grateful that _____ made me laugh today because they_____
_____
I am grateful that I accomplished_____
I am grateful that I had time to_____
I am grateful for overcoming_____
I am grateful that I am_____
I am greatful for the beautiful things I have seen today_____
_____

Lessons I learnt today:

How I shared my gratitude with others today:

Tomorrow I am looking forward to:

I Am Grateful

Date:

My day today was:

People I am grateful for:

The best part of the day was

I am grateful for my friend_____
I am grateful that _____ made me smile today because they_____
_____
I am grateful that _____ made me laugh today because they_____
_____
I am grateful that I accomplished_____
I am grateful that I had time to_____
I am grateful for overcoming_____
I am grateful that I am_____
I am greatful for the beautiful things I have seen today_____
_____

Lessons I learnt today:

How I shared my gratitude with others today:

Tomorrow I am looking forward to:

I Am Grateful

Date:

My day today was:

People I am grateful for:

The best part of the day was

I am grateful for my friend_____

I am grateful that _____ made me smile today because they_____
_____

I am grateful that _____ made me laugh today because they_____
_____

I am grateful that I accomplished_____

I am grateful that I had time to_____

I am grateful for overcoming_____

I am grateful that I am_____

I am greatful for the beautiful things I have seen today_____
_____

Lessons I learnt today:

How I shared my gratitude with others today:

Tomorrow I am looking forward to:

I Am Grateful

Date:

People I am grateful for:

My day today was:

The best part of the day was

I am grateful for my friend_____

I am grateful that _____ made me smile today because they_____

_____

I am grateful that _____ made me laugh today because they_____

_____

I am grateful that I accomplished_____

I am grateful that I had time to_____

I am grateful for overcoming_____

I am grateful that I am_____

I am greatful for the beautiful things I have seen today_____

_____

Lessons I learnt today:

How I shared my gratitude with others today:

Tomorrow I am looking forward to:

I Am Grateful

Date:

My day today was:

People I am grateful for:

The best part of the day was

I am grateful for my friend_____

I am grateful that _____ made me smile today because they_____
_____

I am grateful that _____ made me laugh today because they_____
_____

I am grateful that I accomplished_____

I am grateful that I had time to_____

I am grateful for overcoming_____

I am grateful that I am_____

I am greatful for the beautiful things I have seen today_____
_____

Lessons I learnt today:

How I shared my gratitude with others today:

Tomorrow I am looking forward to:

I Am Grateful

Date:

My day today was:

People I am grateful for:

The best part of the day was

I am grateful for my friend_____
I am grateful that _____ made me smile today because they_____
_____
I am grateful that _____ made me laugh today because they_____
_____

I am grateful that I accomplished_____
I am grateful that I had time to_____
I am grateful for overcoming_____
I am grateful that I am_____
I am greatful for the beautiful things I have seen today_____
_____

Lessons I learnt today:

How I shared my gratitude with others today:

Tomorrow I am looking forward to:

I Am Grateful

Date:

People I am grateful for:

My day today was:

The best part of the day was

I am grateful for my friend_____

I am grateful that _____ made me smile today because they_____
_____

I am grateful that _____ made me laugh today because they_____
_____

I am grateful that I accomplished_____

I am grateful that I had time to_____

I am grateful for overcoming_____

I am grateful that I am_____

I am greatful for the beautiful things I have seen today_____
_____

Lessons I learnt today:

How I shared my gratitude with others today:

Tomorrow I am looking forward to:

I Am Grateful

Date:

My day today was:

People I am grateful for:

The best part of the day was

I am grateful for my friend_____
I am grateful that _____ made me smile today because they_____
_____
I am grateful that _____ made me laugh today because they_____
_____
I am grateful that I accomplished_____
I am grateful that I had time to_____
I am grateful for overcoming_____
I am grateful that I am_____
I am greatful for the beautiful things I have seen today_____
_____

Lessons I learnt today:

How I shared my gratitude with others today:

Tomorrow I am looking forward to:

I Am Grateful

Date:

My day today was:

People I am grateful for:

The best part of the day was

I am grateful for my friend_____

I am grateful that _____ made me smile today because they_____
_____

I am grateful that _____ made me laugh today because they_____
_____

I am grateful that I accomplished_____

I am grateful that I had time to_____

I am grateful for overcoming_____

I am grateful that I am_____

I am greatful for the beautiful things I have seen today_____
_____

Lessons I learnt today:

How I shared my gratitude with others today:

Tomorrow I am looking forward to:

I Am Grateful

Date:

People I am grateful for:

My day today was:

The best part of the day was

I am grateful for my friend_____

I am grateful that _____ made me smile today because they_____

_____

I am grateful that _____ made me laugh today because they_____

_____

I am grateful that I accomplished_____

I am grateful that I had time to_____

I am grateful for overcoming_____

I am grateful that I am_____

I am greatful for the beautiful things I have seen today_____

_____

Lessons I learnt today:

How I shared my gratitude with others today:

Tomorrow I am looking forward to:

I Am Grateful

Date:

My day today was:

People I am grateful for:

The best part of the day was

I am grateful for my friend_____

I am grateful that _____ made me smile today because they_____

_____

I am grateful that _____ made me laugh today because they_____

_____

I am grateful that I accomplished_____

I am grateful that I had time to_____

I am grateful for overcoming_____

I am grateful that I am_____

I am greatful for the beautiful things I have seen today_____

_____

Lessons I learnt today:

How I shared my gratitude with others today:

Tomorrow I am looking forward to:

I Am Grateful

Date:

People I am grateful for:

My day today was:

The best part of the day was

I am grateful for my friend_____

I am grateful that _____ made me smile today because they_____

_____

I am grateful that _____ made me laugh today because they_____

_____

I am grateful that I accomplished_____

I am grateful that I had time to_____

I am grateful for overcoming_____

I am grateful that I am_____

I am greatful for the beautiful things I have seen today_____

_____

Lessons I learnt today:

How I shared my gratitude with others today:

Tomorrow I am looking forward to:

I Am Grateful

Date:

My day today was:

People I am grateful for:

The best part of the day was

I am grateful for my friend_____

I am grateful that _____ made me smile today because they_____

_____

I am grateful that _____ made me laugh today because they_____

_____

I am grateful that I accomplished_____

I am grateful that I had time to_____

I am grateful for overcoming_____

I am grateful that I am_____

I am greatful for the beautiful things I have seen today_____

_____

Lessons I learnt today:

How I shared my gratitude with others today:

Tomorrow I am looking forward to:

I Am Grateful

Date:

My day today was:

People I am grateful for:

The best part of the day was

I am grateful for my friend_____
I am grateful that _____ made me smile today because they_____
_____
I am grateful that _____ made me laugh today because they_____

I am grateful that I accomplished_____
I am grateful that I had time to_____
I am grateful for overcoming_____
I am grateful that I am_____
I am greatful for the beautiful things I have seen today_____

Lessons I learnt today:

How I shared my gratitude with others today:

Tomorrow I am looking forward to:

I Am Grateful

Date:

My day today was:

People I am grateful for:

The best part of the day was

I am grateful for my friend_____

I am grateful that _____ made me smile today because they_____
_____

I am grateful that _____ made me laugh today because they_____
_____

I am grateful that I accomplished_____

I am grateful that I had time to_____

I am grateful for overcoming_____

I am grateful that I am_____

I am greatful for the beautiful things I have seen today_____
_____

Lessons I learnt today:

How I shared my gratitude with others today:

Tomorrow I am looking forward to:

I Am Grateful

Date:

My day today was:

People I am grateful for:

The best part of the day was

I am grateful for my friend_____

I am grateful that _____ made me smile today because they_____
_____

I am grateful that _____ made me laugh today because they_____
_____

I am grateful that I accomplished_____

I am grateful that I had time to_____

I am grateful for overcoming_____

I am grateful that I am_____

I am greatful for the beautiful things I have seen today_____
_____

Lessons I learnt today:

How I shared my gratitude with others today:

Tomorrow I am looking forward to:

I Am Grateful

Date:

My day today was:

People I am grateful for:

The best part of the day was

I am grateful for my friend_____
I am grateful that _____ made me smile today because they_____
_____
I am grateful that _____ made me laugh today because they_____
_____
I am grateful that I accomplished_____
I am grateful that I had time to_____
I am grateful for overcoming_____
I am grateful that I am_____
I am greatful for the beautiful things I have seen today_____
_____

Lessons I learnt today:

How I shared my gratitude with others today:

Tomorrow I am looking forward to:

I Am Grateful

Date:

My day today was:

People I am grateful for:

The best part of the day was

I am grateful for my friend_____

I am grateful that _____ made me smile today because they_____

_____

I am grateful that _____ made me laugh today because they_____

_____

I am grateful that I accomplished_____

I am grateful that I had time to_____

I am grateful for overcoming_____

I am grateful that I am_____

I am greatful for the beautiful things I have seen today_____

_____

Lessons I learnt today:

How I shared my gratitude with others today:

Tomorrow I am looking forward to:

I Am Grateful

Date:

My day today was:

People I am grateful for:

The best part of the day was

I am grateful for my friend_____

I am grateful that _____ made me smile today because they_____

_____

I am grateful that _____ made me laugh today because they_____

_____

I am grateful that I accomplished_____

I am grateful that I had time to_____

I am grateful for overcoming_____

I am grateful that I am_____

I am greatful for the beautiful things I have seen today_____

_____

Lessons I learnt today:

How I shared my gratitude with others today:

Tomorrow I am looking forward to:

I Am Grateful

Date:

People I am grateful for:

My day today was:

The best part of the day was

I am grateful for my friend_____

I am grateful that _____ made me smile today because they_____

_____

I am grateful that _____ made me laugh today because they_____

_____

I am grateful that I accomplished_____

I am grateful that I had time to_____

I am grateful for overcoming_____

I am grateful that I am_____

I am greatful for the beautiful things I have seen today_____

_____

Lessons I learnt today:

How I shared my gratitude with others today:

Tomorrow I am looking forward to:

I Am Grateful

Date:

My day today was:

People I am grateful for:

The best part of the day was

I am grateful for my friend_____
I am grateful that _____ made me smile today because they_____
_____
I am grateful that _____ made me laugh today because they_____
_____
I am grateful that I accomplished_____
I am grateful that I had time to_____
I am grateful for overcoming_____
I am grateful that I am_____
I am greatful for the beautiful things I have seen today_____
_____

Lessons I learnt today:

How I shared my gratitude with others today:

Tomorrow I am looking forward to:

I Am Grateful

Date:

People I am grateful for:

My day today was:

The best part of the day was

I am grateful for my friend_____

I am grateful that _____ made me smile today because they_____

_____

I am grateful that _____ made me laugh today because they_____

_____

I am grateful that I accomplished_____

I am grateful that I had time to_____

I am grateful for overcoming_____

I am grateful that I am_____

I am greatful for the beautiful things I have seen today_____

_____

Lessons I learnt today:

How I shared my gratitude with others today:

Tomorrow I am looking forward to:

I Am Grateful

Date:

My day today was:

People I am grateful for:

The best part of the day was

I am grateful for my friend_____

I am grateful that _____ made me smile today because they_____
_____

I am grateful that _____ made me laugh today because they_____
_____

I am grateful that I accomplished_____

I am grateful that I had time to_____

I am grateful for overcoming_____

I am grateful that I am_____

I am greatful for the beautiful things I have seen today_____
_____

Lessons I learnt today:

How I shared my gratitude with others today:

Tomorrow I am looking forward to:

I Am Grateful

Date:

My day today was:

People I am grateful for:

The best part of the day was

I am grateful for my friend_____

I am grateful that _____ made me smile today because they_____
_____

I am grateful that _____ made me laugh today because they_____
_____

I am grateful that I accomplished_____

I am grateful that I had time to_____

I am grateful for overcoming_____

I am grateful that I am_____

I am greatful for the beautiful things I have seen today_____
_____

Lessons I learnt today:

How I shared my gratitude with others today:

Tomorrow I am looking forward to:

I Am Grateful

Date:

People I am grateful for:

My day today was:

The best part of the day was

I am grateful for my friend_____

I am grateful that _____ made me smile today because they_____
_____

I am grateful that _____ made me laugh today because they_____

_____

I am grateful that I accomplished_____

I am grateful that I had time to_____

I am grateful for overcoming_____

I am grateful that I am_____

I am greatful for the beautiful things I have seen today_____
_____

Lessons I learnt today:

How I shared my gratitude with others today:

Tomorrow I am looking forward to:

I Am Grateful

Date:

My day today was:

People I am grateful for:

The best part of the day was

I am grateful for my friend_____
I am grateful that _____ made me smile today because they_____
_____
I am grateful that _____ made me laugh today because they_____

I am grateful that I accomplished_____
I am grateful that I had time to_____
I am grateful for overcoming_____
I am grateful that I am_____
I am greatful for the beautiful things I have seen today_____
_____

Lessons I learnt today:

How I shared my gratitude with others today:

Tomorrow I am looking forward to:

I Am Grateful

Date:

My day today was:

People I am grateful for:

The best part of the day was

I am grateful for my friend_____

I am grateful that _____ made me smile today because they_____

_____

I am grateful that _____ made me laugh today because they_____

_____

I am grateful that I accomplished_____

I am grateful that I had time to_____

I am grateful for overcoming_____

I am grateful that I am_____

I am greatful for the beautiful things I have seen today_____

_____

Lessons I learnt today:

How I shared my gratitude with others today:

Tomorrow I am looking forward to:

Made in the USA
Monee, IL
07 May 2021